To Benjamin, Henry and Mary Margaret Barnes —
the three precious children who call me Grammie and
bring me untold joy. May you grow up to trust Jesus as
Lord and *Do Great Things for God!*

"I love this book. As a pastor's wife who has daily health struggles like Susanna Spurgeon, I love how this book highlights how God does great things even in those who struggle with much weakness. There is no one whom God saves that he does not use. And sometimes in ways far more than they could ever imagine."

CONNIE DEVER, Pastor's Wife, Capitol Hill Baptist Church, Washington, D.C.

"Susannah Spurgeon's story is a great one to tell, and Mary Mohler is a great author to tell it. I heartily recommend this book."

JASON K. ALLEN, President, Midwestern Baptist Theological Seminary and Spurgeon College

"A sweet way to introduce children to the concept of quiet faithfulness and the joy that comes from loving Jesus, caring for family, and serving his church."

ERIN ROBERTSON, Children's Ministry Coordinator, Third Avenue Baptist Church, Louisville, KY

"Susannah Spurgeon is a wonderful example for young girls. Mary captures Susannah's spirit of love, devotion, and determination to use her life for good, even when life is hard."

ANN IORG, President's Wife, Gateway Seminary of the SBC

"As a mother of daughters and educator of future teachers, I can't wait to share this book with them and encourage them to use their time in a way that best serves God."

WHITNEY BRUCE, Adjunct Instructor of Teacher Education, Boyce College

"A must-read for those teaching children about the beauty of biblical womanhood and the sovereignty of God."

ELLIE COURSEY, Children's Ministry Director, Henderson's First Baptist Church, Kentucky

Susannah Spurgeon
© Mary K. Mohler 2024

Illustrated by Cecilia Messina | Design and Art Direction by André Parker
Series Concept by Laura Caputo-Wickham

"The Good Book For Children" is an imprint of The Good Book Company Ltd.
thegoodbook.com | thegoodbook.co.uk | thegoodbook.com.au
thegoodbook.co.nz | thegoodbook.co.in

ISBN: 9781784989750 | JOB-007656 | Printed in India

thegoodbook
for children

Do Great Things for God

Inspiring Biographies for Young Children

Do Great Things for God
Corrie ten Boom
The Courageous Woman and the Secret Room
Laura Caputo-Wickham
Illustrated by Isabel Muñoz

Do Great Things for God
Betsey Stockton
The Girl With a Missionary Dream
Laura Caputo-Wickham
Illustrated by Eunji Jung

Do Great Things for God
Queen Elizabeth II
The Queen Who Chose to Serve
Alison Mitchell
Illustrated by Emma Randall

Do Great Things for God
Helen Roseveare
The Doctor Who Kept Going No Matter What
Laura Caputo-Wickham
Illustrated by Cecilia Messina

Do Great Things for God
Gladys Aylward
The Little Woman With a Big Dream
Laura Caputo-Wickham
Illustrated by Jess Rose

Do Great Things for God
Betty Greene
The Girl Who Longed to Fly
Laura Caputo-Wickham
Illustrated by Héloïse Mab

Do Great Things for God
Fanny Crosby
The Girl Who Couldn't See but Helped the World to Sing
Laura Caputo-Wickham
Illustrated by Jess Rose

Do Great Things for God
Fannie Lou Hamer
The Courageous Woman Who Marched for Dignity
K. A. Ellis
Illustrated by Shin Maeng

Do Great Things for God
Maria Fearing
The Girl Who Dreamed of Distant Lands
K. A. Ellis
Illustrated by Isabel Muñoz

Do Great Things for God
Amy Carmichael
The Brown-eyed Girl Who Learned to Pray
Hunter Beless
Illustrated by Héloïse Mab

Do Great Things for God
Susannah Spurgeon
The Pastor's Wife Who Didn't Let Sickness Stop Her
Mary K. Mohler
Illustrated by Cecilia Messina

thegoodbook.com | thegoodbook.co.uk

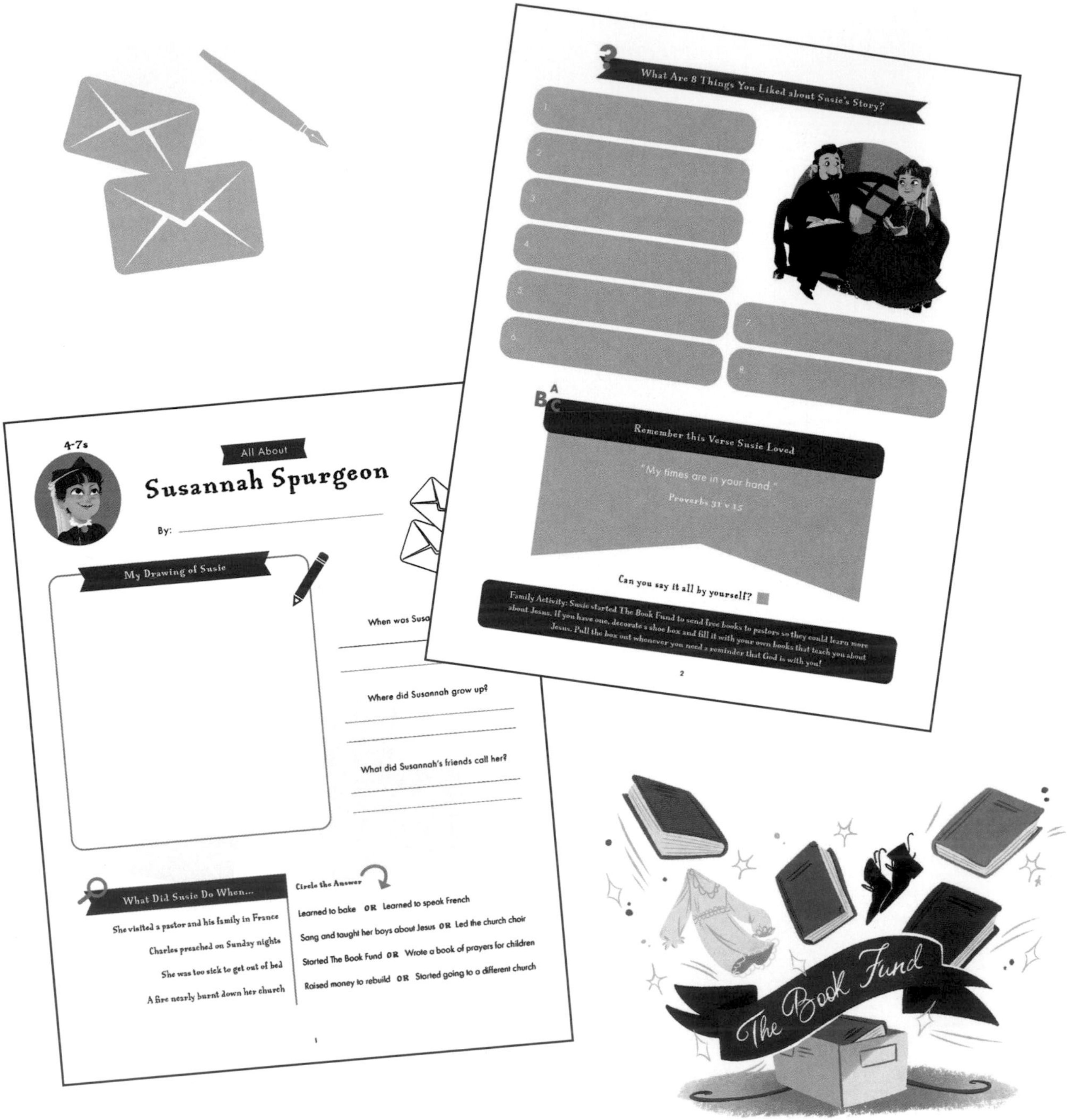

1.
2.
3.
4.
5.
6.
7.
8.

Remember this Verse Susie Loved

"My times are in your hand."

Proverbs 31 v 15

Can you say it all by yourself? ☐

Family Activity: Susie started The Book Fund to send free books to pastors so they could learn more about Jesus. If you have one, decorate a shoe box and fill it with your own books that teach you about Jesus. Pull the box out whenever you need a reminder that God is with you!

2

4-7s

All About

Susannah Spurgeon

By: _____

My Drawing of Susie

When was Susa...

Where did Susannah grow up?

What did Susannah's friends call her?

What Did Susie Do When...   Circle the Answer

She visited a pastor and his family in France   Learned to bake OR Learned to speak French

Charles preached on Sunday nights   Sang and taught her boys about Jesus OR Led the church choir

She was too sick to get out of bed   Started The Book Fund OR Wrote a book of prayers for children

A fire nearly burnt down her church   Raised money to rebuild OR Started going to a different church

1

The Book Fund

Download Free Resources at

thegoodbook.com/kids-resources

Interact With Susie's Story!

Biography Report for
Susannah Spurgeon

By: _____

My favorite thing about Susie:
_____
_____

Person from the Bible Susie reminds me of:
_____
_____

A question I would ask Susie:
_____
_____
_____

Three words I would use to describe Susie:

1. _____
2. _____
3. _____

Remember this Verse Susie Loved

"My _____ are _____;

your _____."

Proverbs 31 v 15

Can you say it 5 times without looking? ☐

· PASSPORT ·

Susannah Spurgeon

Year of Birth:

Hometown:

Nickname:

[Draw a Portrait]

Search Online to Find:
Ask an adult about doing this together!

Susie started The Book Fund to send Charles' books to pastors who couldn't afford them. Name a few of the books that she sent out.
_____
_____
_____

List 3 books Susie wrote.
_____
_____
_____

Read a few of Susie and Charles' letters. Write a line or two that shows how much they loved Jesus and each other.
_____
_____
_____

Tell Susie's story in your own words. You can even pretend you are Susie and say "I", thinking about how she might feel.

_____
_____
_____
_____
_____
_____
_____
_____
_____
_____

Can you put these events in order? Number the boxes from 1 to 6.

☐ Susie gave birth to twin boys

☐ Susie raised money to rebuild her church after it nearly burned down

☐ Susie learned to speak French

☐ Susie and Charles both became ill

☐ Susie and Charles got married

☐ Susie started The Book Fund to send free books to pastors

Family Activity: Not every family can send free books to pastors and missionaries, but many of us can send letters! Write a letter or two of encouragement and send it to a pastor or missionary from your church, or search online for organizations that can send your letter on to a missionary for you.

Dear Wifey,

Precious Husband

NORTH
AMERICA

EUROP

England

SOUTH
AMERICA

World Map

Where in the world
did Susie's story
take place?

31 January 1892 Charles Spurgeon died while by the sea in France.

1895 Susie helped raise money to build a Baptist church at Bexhill-on-Sea.

1896, 1898 and 1901 Susie's three devotional books were published.

20 April 1898 The Metropolitan Tabernacle was badly damaged by a fire. Susie helped raise money to rebuild it.

22 October 1903 Susie died at home and was buried in London next to her husband.

Susannah Spurgeon

15 January 1832 Susannah Thompson was born in London, England. She was known as Susie.

18 December 1853 Susie heard Charles Spurgeon preach at New Park Street Chapel.

4 February 1855 Susie was baptized by Charles Spurgeon.

8 January 1856 Charles and Susie were married and took a wedding trip to France.

7 October 1857 Charles preached to 24,000 people at the Crystal Palace.

18 March 1861 The new church, Metropolitan Tabernacle, opened and could seat 6,000 people.

1868 Susie's sickness got worse. She had surgery but was no longer able to travel.

1872 Charles' health got worse, and he often had to leave London to get better.

1875 Susie started the Book Fund, a project to send copies of Charles' books to poor pastors. She sent about 200,000 books in all.

Questions to Think About

1. Which part of Susie's story did you like best?

2. Even though she was sick, Susie asked God to give her good work to do. Is there anything that makes it hard for you to do good work? Maybe, like Susie, you're sick. Or maybe where you live or how young you are makes it hard. Ask God to show you how you can serve him, even if that seems difficult.

3. When Susie heard that many poor pastors could not afford books, she started the Book Fund. Can you think of a person or group that doesn't have as much as you have? What could you do to help them?

4. What ideas does Susie's story give you about how you might serve Jesus when you are older?

5. What is one truth about God that you'd like to remember from this story?

Susannah Spurgeon

1832 – 1903

"My times are in your hand."

Psalm 31:15

Susie was married to a very gifted man of God who preached to millions of people about Jesus. But he could not have done what he did without his wonderful wife, who encouraged him like no one else could.

Susie did not let sickness mean she pulled up the bed covers and felt sorry for herself. She studied her Bible and prayed daily.

Susie knew that her times were in God's hand. She asked God to give her good work to do— and he did!

Susie spent some time near the sea at the end of her life.
Since there was not a Baptist church there, Susie asked
people to give money so that one could be started.
Many did, and a church was built. Beulah Baptist Church
still meets there today.

Charles had served as a pastor for nearly 40 years. Charles and Susie's son Thomas became the next pastor of the church.

But soon, a great fire nearly destroyed it!

Susie encouraged people to give money so that it could be rebuilt.

Susie missed him greatly but knew she would be with him forever in heaven. She continued her work as best she could.

The twin boys were both married. Susie enjoyed being called Grandmama by her six grandchildren. She was happy to have all of her family close by.

Despite his illness, Charles continued to preach and teach. But he didn't get better, and when Susie was 60, Charles died.

They sent about 200,000 books in all. What a wonderful way to help so many pastors! Charles was proud of her for all she did even while she was sick.

Susie knew that many pastors were poor and had no way to buy any of the books written by Charles. So Susie had a great idea to help them without leaving home!

She called it the Book Fund.

The Book Fund

Susie and her friends asked others to give money to the Book Fund. They packaged up the books and sent them all over the country. They sent clothing and shoes to some families too.

But Susie too was sick. She had to stay in bed and could not make the long trips with Charles. There were no phones then, so they could only write letters to each other.

Dear Wifey,

Precious Husband,

Susie continued to pray for strength and for good work to do even when she was too sick to leave home.

God answered her prayer...

Sometimes, Charles would have to travel to the sea in France in order to get away from the thick smoke in the air in the big city of London. He would have to stay by the sea for many weeks until he could breathe better.

But Susie became very sick and had to stay in bed for much of the time. Charles was also very sick at times. This was very hard for this young family.

Susie did the best she could every day. She often read the verse in the Bible that says:

"My times are in your hand." (Psalm 31:15)

Susie knew that her times were safely in God's hand, whether she was sick or well.

She prayed for strength and for good work to do even when she was too sick to leave home.

On Saturday nights, Susie helped her husband in his study as he prepared his sermon for Sunday.

Charles became the most famous pastor of his day.
He traveled by horse and carriage to preach all over
England and Wales about ten times per week—
and then preached at his church on Sunday as well.

The Spurgeons had twin boys, Charles and Thomas. Susie was a busy pastor's wife who enjoyed helping her husband and taking care of their baby boys.

On Sunday nights, while Charles was preaching at church, Susie would stay home and teach the twins about Jesus. They sat at the piano bench together as she played hymns, and they all sang with happy hearts.

Charles and Susie enjoyed getting to know each other. They fell in love, and Charles asked Susie to marry him just a few months after they met. They were married about a year and a half later.

But then Susie met the pastor, and they became friends. She saw how kind he was and how he loved to teach the Bible.

He helped her to understand how amazing our God is.

Susie became a Christian.

But Susie thought he sounded funny and dressed sloppily. She was not very interested in what he had to say... at first.

Back in London, when she was 21, Susie and her family visited a church to hear Charles Spurgeon preach. Everyone seemed to love his preaching.

Susannah Thompson was born in London, England. She was known as Susie to her friends.

Susie did not have any brothers or sisters. She enjoyed learning to play the piano and reading books.

Susie often took exciting trips to France to visit a pastor and his family. She enjoyed going to the beautiful museums there. The pastor's daughters taught Susie how to speak French.

Susannah Spurgeon

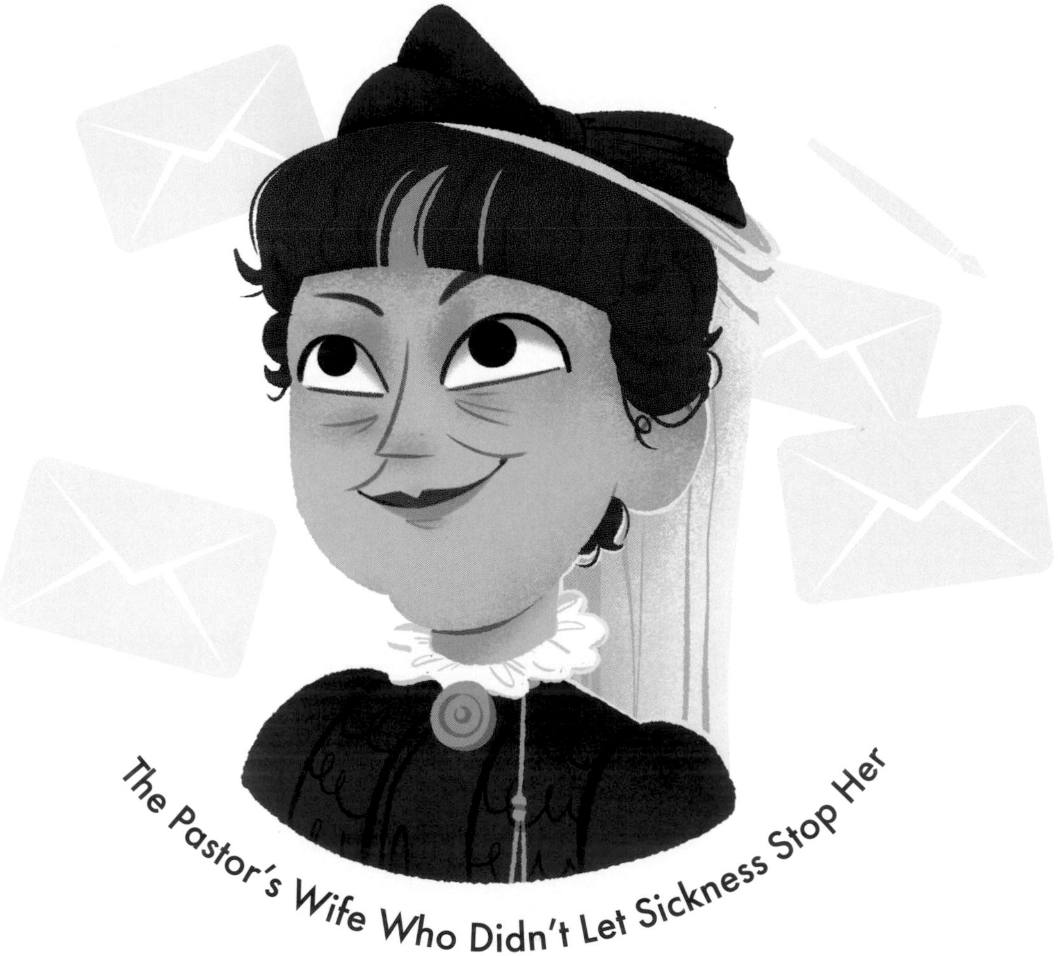

The Pastor's Wife Who Didn't Let Sickness Stop Her

Mary K. Mohler

Illustrated by Cecilia Messina